THE SCARBOROUGH & WHITBY RA

A PHOTOGRAPHIC & HISTORICAL SURVEY BY J. ROBIN

CW00405489

1. Falsgrave, Scarborough, in 1952 looking from Westwood wall towards the Central station. The Scarborough & Whitby Railway commenced by a junction with the York-Scarborough line, below the wall of the former Quaker burial ground on the left, and proceeded almost immediately through the tunnel to Gallows Close. To the right of the tunnel, in front of the signal box, is platform 1A which was built in 1934 to ease congestion in the station. Prior to this date coast line trains departed, in the summer months, from the platforms on the south side of the station. They then had to cross the main lines (in the foreground) thereby interrupting the heavy traffic in and out of the Central station.

First Edition, June 1977   Second Impression, April 1980   Third Impression, May 1981
Fourth Impression, April 1983   Fifth Impression, April 1984   Sixth Impression, May 1993

Published by: Hendon Publishing Company, Hendon Mill, Nelson, Lancashire.
© J. Robin Lidster, 1977
Printed by Peter Fretwell & Sons Ltd., Healey Works, Goulbourne Street, Keighley, West Yorkshire BD21 1PZ.

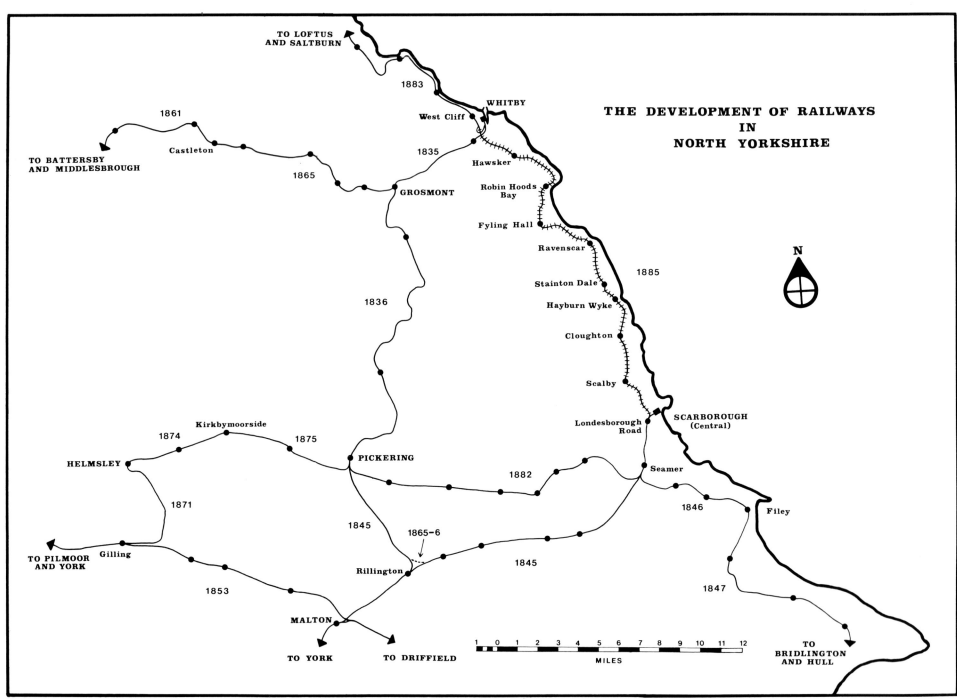

TO LOFTUS
AND SALTBURN

1883

WHITBY

West Cliff

1861

Castleton

TO BATTERSBY
AND MIDDLESBROUGH

1865

1835

Hawsker

Robin Hoods
Bay

GROSMONT

Fyling Hall

Ravenscar

1885

1836

Stainton Dale

Hayburn Wyke

Cloughton

Scalby

Kirkbymoorside

Londesborough
Road

SCARBOROUGH
(Central)

1874

1875

HELMSLEY

PICKERING

1882

Seamer

1871

1845

1865-6

1846

Filey

TO PILMOOR
AND YORK

Gilling

Rillington

1845

1853

1847

MALTON

TO YORK

TO DRIFFIELD

THE DEVELOPMENT OF RAILWAYS
IN
NORTH YORKSHIRE

N

1 0 1 2 3 4 5 6 7 8 9 10 11 12
MILES

TO
BRIDLINGTON
AND HULL

THE SCARBOROUGH & WHITBY RAILWAY was opened on 16th July 1885, long after the period of "railway mania" shattered the rural peace of England in the 1840's. The first suggestion to link the two towns by rail came in 1848, three years after the opening of the York-Scarborough line which also branched out at Rillington to connect up to the hitherto independent Whitby-Pickering line, opened throughout in 1836.

This first scheme came under the title of the Scarborough, Whitby, Stockton on Tees & Newcastle & North Junction Railway about which very little is known. No reasons are recorded for its proposal but the period of railway mania was noted for its lack of reason when many wildly impractical schemes were proposed. The SWS on T&N&NJR was undoubtedly one of these, not least for the length of its initials!

Looked at in practical terms the topography between Scarborough and Whitby is not the easiest of terrain for railway engineering. Bounded on the east by a rugged coast line, the hinterland rises to more than 800 feet, with Ravenscar roughly half way between the two. Without spending an irrecoverable fortune on building a railway there are only three possible routes: all were suggested in the 1860's, with variations, and detailed plans were executed.

In 1863 a line under the title of the Scarborough, Whitby & Staithes Railway was proposed. This had the backing of the then independent Cleveland Railway Company who wished to extend their railway southwards along the coast from Loftus to Scarborough. This would have taken traffic away from the giant North Eastern Railway Company which had had the virtual monopoly of rail traffic in the area from 1854. It was this proposal, together with other considerations, which led the NER to open negotiations with the Cleveland Railway board and the SW&SR proposal was dropped.

The railway was to have commenced in Falsgrave, close to the Quaker burial ground, which is in fact where the final scheme was to start. The line was then to run northwards, passing east of Scalby, Burniston and Cloughton, to Staintondale where it was to pass through a tunnel on to Beast Cliff at Petard Point. Beast Cliff is in fact an undercliff—a shelf of rock formed by the differential weathering of two different types of strata—situated about half way down the 400 feet high cliff. This feature continues up to Peak (Ravenscar) where the railway was to skirt perilously round into Robin Hood's Bay. The course of the line was then to continue round the bay within half a mile of the cliffs and would have entailed some considerable engineering works, in the form of heavy embankments or long viaducts, to cross the deep wooded valleys which traverse this area. North of Robin Hood's Bay the route would have been similar to that actually built, although the river Esk at Whitby was to have been crossed at a much lower level by a three-span viaduct 280 feet long. The maximum altitude of 315 feet would have been reached near Hawsker. The cost of the scheme was estimated at £450,000 but there was little public interest in it and it was opposed by the NER.

The SW&SR proposal, although an early failure, did rekindle interest in the possibility of connecting the two towns and in 1864 three more plans were put forward. The first was based upon the previous scheme and proposed by a Mr. Climie, a Scarborough resident, who suggested that a narrow gauge tramway should be built to Cloughton. This, he said, could run up the high road, be horse-worked, and convey both passengers and goods. The cost was estimated at a mere £13,000, but it could later be converted to a locomotive worked line if the income warranted such a development.

The second suggestion of 1864 was promoted by a Mr. Bartholomew, of Doncaster, whose plan for a direct mineral line was to cost £150,000. The line was to commence by a junction with the NER south-west of what was later to become the site of Londesborough Road excursion station. The route then passed west of the villages of Scalby and Burniston to Harwood Dale, where it climbed over the moors into the head of Iburndale and so down to connect with the NER at Sleights. The railway was intended to be a surface line involving few cuttings or embankments but following the natural rise and fall of the ground. Its purpose was to exploit the mineral resources of the area: limestone around Hackness and ironstone in Iburndale. Certainly this was the shortest connecting route, but, with a summit at 700 feet and a constant rising gradient of 1 in 50 for six miles for southbound trains, it was a rather impractical proposition.

The third scheme of 1864 received by far the greater support; this was for a coast line route, a Bill for which was put before Parliament. This was approved and the Act received the Royal Assent on 5th July 1865. The document runs to 15 pages of closely printed foolscap which, for the first time, authorised the incorporation of a Scarborough & Whitby Railway Company with a capital not to exceed £275,000 in ten pound shares. One clause in the Act required the company to expend the money raised in constructing simultaneously the sections of the line from Whitby to Peak and Scarborough to Peak. William Henry Hammond of Raven Hall at Peak was named as one of the first directors and he was later to be referred to as "the father of the railway".

The line was to have commenced at Scarborough by a similar junction and at the same place as that proposed for the Iburndale scheme. The route was then similar to that proposed for the SW&SR of 1863 in that it was to emerge through a tunnel on to Beast Cliff. The railway was to terminate by a junction with the NER, half way between Ruswarp and Sleights, on the south side of the river Esk. The Act stipulated that the railway was to be completed in five years.

The NER considered the making of a direct line was not a necessity (they had a service via Malton!) and presented a petition to Parliament against the scheme. This did not deter the promotors who issued a Prospectus in

June 1865 which stated that the object of the railway was to shorten the distance by rail between the two towns from 56 miles (by the NER route) down to 19 miles, and to develop the abundant mineral resources of the district. Rather optimistically it was stated that there were extensive seams of ironstone, best quality freestone (for building), dogger or Roman cement stone, blue lias limestone, alum rock, hard and soft jet, whinstone, firebrick clay etc.

A direct result of this proposal was the construction by the NER of the Rillington junction curve (see map). On the first of July 1865 express trains commenced running for the first time between Scarborough and Whitby, taking 1½ hours. The curve closed the following year, due to a severe depression in the North of England, and it never reopened.

In April 1865 it was reported that the S&WR engineer (Eugenius Birch) and the contractor (W. Tredwell) had gone over the route again and were pleased with it. Hopes of starting the work in August were dashed as sufficient capital was not forthcoming and nothing more was heard of the S&WR until 1870.

In this year yet another plan emerged, completely different from the previous scheme, for an isolated line of railway from Scarborough to Whitby. The line was to be about 20 miles long, commencing in a piece of ground at Scarborough called Gallows Close and terminating by a 1 in 5½ incline down to Gideons timber pond on the Esk at Whitby. Here the Act, which obtained the Royal Assent on 29th June 1871, authorised the S&WR to build all proper wharfs, shipping and landing places. The capital was to be £120,000 and W. H. Hammond was again named as one of the directors. The powers for the compulsory purchase of land were to expire in 1874 and the line was to be completed in 1876.

Active operations were commenced on Monday the 3rd of June 1872 when a party of excavators opened the ground at a point near Scarborough cemetery. The contractors were Kirk & Parry and the engineer was again Eugenius Birch. By August 1873 the first seven miles at the Scarborough end were ready for the ballast and permanent way whilst the Whitby end had been staked out but the land, at that time, had not been purchased.

It had been realised in the previous year that junctions would be needed at both ends of the line if the undertaking was to be a viable proposition. A Bill for these was put to Parliament and obtained the Royal Assent on 26th May 1873. This Act authorised the construction of the necessary works including the tunnel at Scarborough, and allowed the raising of a further £40,000 capital.

Progress from this time (1873) was exceedingly slow and eventually the company could raise no more capital, whilst considerable sums were owing to the engineer, contractor and other parties, so that by 1877 a complete standstill had been reached. It was then suggested by some of the shareholders that a Receiver should be called in and the company wound up. No action was taken and new hopes were raised in 1878 when a contractor from Manchester, a Mr. James Evans, offered to take over the liabilities of the company and complete the line on favourable terms. That offer was made before he had gone over the line—afterwards a pair of very cold Mancunian feet could have been seen disappearing rapidly westwards!

The affairs again lapsed into a dormant state until in 1879 fresh efforts were made to have the line completed. A Bill was put before Parliament to revive the powers of the 1871 and 1873 Acts and to extend the periods for the purchase of land and completion of the railway. The Act allowed the capital to be increased by a further £80,000 to a total of £240,000 and the Royal Assent was given on the 12th August 1880. New engineers were appointed—Sir Charles Fox & Sons of Westminster—and they estimated that it would cost £157,187 to complete the line. Tenders were invited and six were received varying from £117,824 up to £157,740. The tender from John Waddell & Son of Edinburgh (£155,822) was accepted and they became the new contractors for the S&WR.

A fresh start was made by Waddell in 1881 and, during the first week of June, the approach of the line into Scarborough was staked out from the termination of the previous efforts near Wrea Lane (Manor Road) to the south end of Gallows Close where the tunnel was to commence.

Details of some of the more notable events which took place during the course of construction will be found accompanying the photographs, which are arranged in topographical order from Scarborough to Whitby. To deal with the 80 years of the line's working history would take far more space than is available in the whole of the present work but a summary of the most important occurrences follows:

From the opening on 16th July 1885 the line was operated by the NER under the Working Agreement dated the 19th September 1884. This contained 23 Articles defining the two companies' interests in the line. Their interpretation of these articles led the S&WR to take the NER to Arbitration in 1888 complaining that they had:

1) Refused to afford all traffic over the line the reasonable facility of through tickets, carriages and wagons

2) Failed to advertise the coast route in a reasonable manner

3) Unreasonably competed with the S&WR by diverting traffic consigned by the coast route over the NER route

4) Fixed unreasonably high charges for traffic over the line

5) Withheld facilities from traders wanting to use the railway

6) Failed to employ the line to its utmost carrying capacity.

Up until that time these grievances had been the subject of an endless stream of letters to Henry Tennant the General Manager of the NER, so much so that in an interview with a representative of the S&WR Tennant said "No good could come to the company (the S&WR) from the present constant correspondence carried on by Mr. Fearnley (the S&WR secretary) which was only irritating and which was becoming intolerable". He added that in his experience of some 35 years he had never known anything like it before.

In 1892 the tables were turned: for some time the NER had been complaining that the S&WR line had not been completed according to the articles of the Working Agreement and they delivered a Schedule of Unfinished Works to the company. This included additions and alterations estimated at a total of £4,710. Amongst the work required to be done were alterations to make Robin Hood's Bay and Cloughton stations into complete passing places. The S&W company signed an agreement to pay for this work on 9th August 1892.

The S&WR was not a profitable line from the outset, partly due to the antagonism that existed between the two companies but principally because of the vast amount of capital that had been expended. This amounted to £649,813—equivalent to £27,000 per mile. The NER decided to buy the line in 1897 after working it at a loss for 50% of the gross receipts. The purchase went through on 1st July 1898 when they acquired the undertaking for a total of £261,333 paid in NER stock.

In the early 1930's traffic improved considerably with the introduction of cheap fares, including the 10/– weekly holiday contract tickets, and a greater number of people travelled over the line than ever before.

Prior to 1933 trains were run over the coast line either between Scarborough and Whitby or between Scarborough and Saltburn but in that year Middlesbrough took over as the northern terminus. This meant that through trains were working a 58 mile run, 37 miles of which was single track, with limited passing places. The gradients were also amongst the most severe in the North Eastern area and the presence of frequent sea frets, which made the rails slippery, aggravated the problem.

In 1933 traffic was so heavy in the summer that great difficulty was experienced in working the service and a Committee on the Working of the Coast Line was set up. Their brief was to make recommendations to give a greatly improved service in the summer of 1934. The Committee visited every station to discuss the working difficulties and their suggestions included the provision of passing places at Hawsker and Fyling Hall, improved signalling at Prospect Hill (near Whitby) and their most brilliant inspiration, the making of a bay platform (1A) in the end of platform 1 at Scarborough Central. The passing places were deferred but the last two recommendations were implemented, the latter with far reaching effects (see title page).

The increase in traffic was short lived, and was in any case only seasonal, and after the second world war, with the rapid expansion of road traffic, the line once more subsided into unprofitability. It was inevitable that the railway would be closed and an example of the financial situation in 1964 gives good reason; during one week in the summer £160 was paid out in wages to the staff of Staintondale and Cloughton who also managed the then unstaffed Hayburn Wyke station. The income from passenger traffic for the three stations in the same week was £6! This is not to say that the whole line was unprofitable: certain aspects were very remunerative, such as the Camping Coaches, but these were insufficient to carry the loss for the whole line.

The withdrawal of goods traffic took place on 4th August 1964 and the last passenger train ran from Scarborough to Whitby on the evening of the 6th March 1965.

Many people, holidaymakers and residents alike, regretted the closure of the line but there is no doubt that in the form in which it then existed it was not financially viable. Perhaps, with hindsight, and from pecuniary considerations only, it should never have been built. Initially, however, it opened up a countryside that had been virtually inaccessible to most people and for 80 years it gave many thousands the opportunity to see and stay in the most picturesque part of the Yorkshire coast.

SCARBOROUGH AND WHITBY RAILWAY. COAST ROUTE.

OFFICIAL GUIDE.

ROBIN HOOD'S BAY.

ROBIN HOOD'S BAY.

2. Left: The cover of the second edition of the Official Scarborough & Whitby Railway Guide published in 1894. There is heavy emphasis on Robin Hood's Bay although the guide contains information about, and suggested walks from, all the villages served by the line—Scalby, Cloughton, Hayburn Wyke, Stainton Dale, Peak (Ravenscar), Fyling Hall, Robin Hood's Bay and Hawsker. The back cover bears a full page advertisement for plots of land on the Mount Pleasant estate at Robin Hood's Bay which was being developed at this time (see reference 40—two photographs).

3. Right: Class J25 locomotive, number 2129, about to enter the south end of Falsgrave tunnel (extreme right) in the early 1920's. The signalman is holding the pouch which contains the single line tablet. This is in effect a key which is used to unlock the signal and point levers for the sections between adjacent signal boxes. Only one tablet for each section may be out at a time which ensures that there can be only one locomotive or train on the single track.

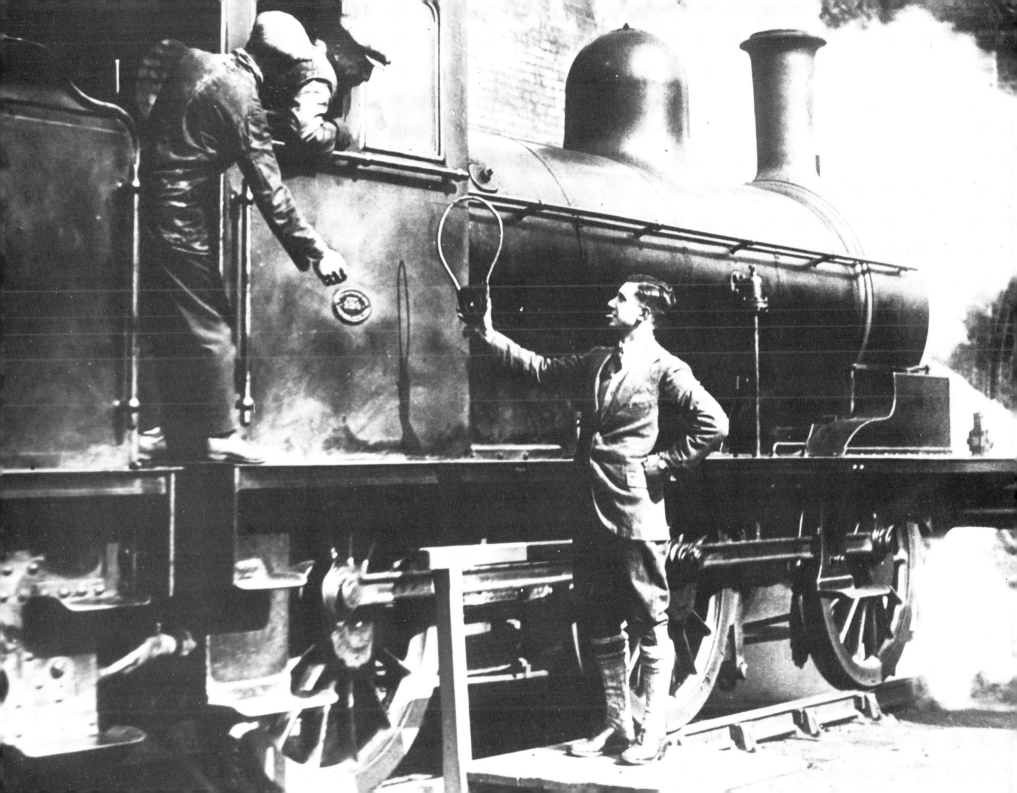

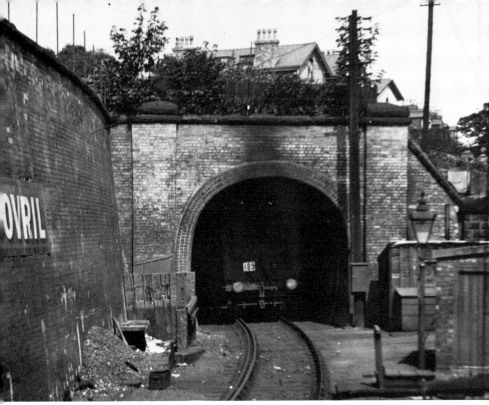

4. Top left: The south portal of Falsgrave tunnel which was built by the cut and cover method, whereby a cutting was excavated and the brickwork formed and then covered over. The Act of Parliament stated that there must be at least two feet of earth above the apex of the tunnel which is 260 yards long. The brickwork was commenced in August 1882 and the first permanent rails were laid here on the 24th March 1883. At the same time it was reported that four shiploads of best Baltic redwood sleepers and nearly 50 trucks of rails and cast iron chairs had arrived. The tunnel was completed in June 1883.

5. Bottom left: Gallows Close in 1961. A departing goods train, hauled by Ivatt 'Mogul' class locomotive 43077, approaches the northern end of Falsgrave tunnel. It was near this point in April 1885, where a number of navvies were excavating, that a man was killed by a fall of clay. This was not the first death of an employee on the line—altogether seven men were killed during the construction of the railway. Most were caused by falls of clay in the cuttings.

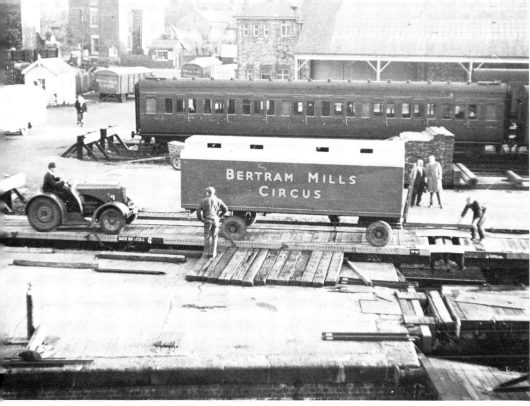

6. Top left: The south end of Gallows Close looking south-west from the wall on the right of the previous photograph. This is one of the more unusual loading operations to take place here—the embarkation of Bertram Mill's Circus, once a regular visitor to Scarborough. The manoeuvre called for some careful driving by the tractorman if he was not to incur the voluble wrath of some of the larger and more ferocious occupants.

The goods shed in the background was opened in 1902 when the NER completed the expansion of the goods yard. The buildings measure 250 feet by 112 feet and were built by Messrs R. Blackett & Son of Darlington at a cost of £9,000.

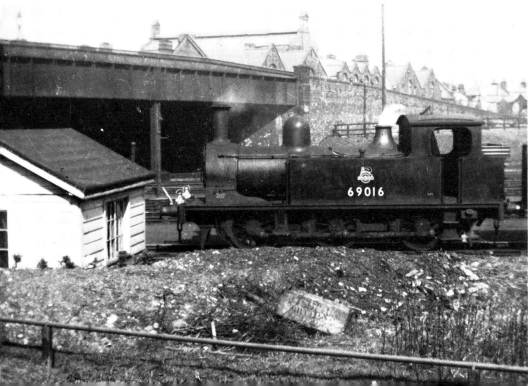

7. Bottom left: A class J72 locomotive acting as goods yard pilot. For many years a locomotive, usually a small tank engine, was used at Gallows Close to perform the various shunting duties. This particular class was designed in 1898 by the NER and was built at varying times over a span of 54 years, the last being built by British Railways in 1951.

On the left is Wykeham Street bridge built in 1896, (superseding the one in photograph 11) which was recently demolished and replaced by a shorter-spanned structure of brick and concrete. The bridge had decayed badly because of locomotives having to stand beneath it to take water from the supply at the western end. When the road surface was scraped off, during demolition, it was found that the inch thick steel plates underneath looked more like chicken netting and one of the contractors' vehicles almost fell through.

9

8. Left: A Sentinel-Cammell steam rail car below the west end of Wykeham Street bridge. These vehicles had a vertical coal-fired boiler at the front and were driven by either 2, 6 or 12 cylinders. The various types were all tried out on the York-Whitby-Scarborough-York route which took in the steepest gradients and the tightest curves in the area. They could be driven from either end and were introduced to replace the autocars which were withdrawn in the late 1920's.

This photograph was taken on the 6th April 1927 on the occasion of such a test and shows the party of officials who travelled on the rail car.

9. Top right: Gallows Close yard looking south from Wykeham Street bridge. In the distance, above and slightly to the left of the locomotive chimney, can be seen the northern end of the Falsgrave tunnel. The goods shed opened in 1902 by the NER is on the right.

Gallows Close was originally intended as the site for the terminal station of the S&WR line but this was rendered unneccessary by the Working Agreement of 1884 whereby the NER agreed to provide terminal accommodation for passenger and goods traffic at Central station.

During the construction of the railway the contractors, John Waddell & Son, used the site as a base for their operations and they put in three or four sidings for their own use. After the line was opened Waddell wished to purchase the site in order to open a goods station. This was very much in his own interest as he owned more than half of the S&W undertaking by way of Lloyds Bonds, stocks and shares to a total of £361,000. It was therefore vital to him to develop traffic on the line but the move was blocked by the NER which eventually, after lengthy High Court proceedings, purchased the site under compulsory purchase powers in 1891. The sidings seen here were laid down by them in 1900.

10. Bottom right: Motive power on the S&WR has varied considerably over the years but ordinary passenger traffic was usually hauled by a variety of tank locomotives. In the early 1900's the existing engine power was found to be insufficient for the special requirements of the line and the class 'W' locomotives were designed by Wilson Worsdell for the coast route. The locomotive seen here is in its original form as built in 1907/8. Ten were built but it was not long before the small coal bunker of only $2\frac{1}{4}$ tons capacity was found to be inadequate. They were then rebuilt between 1915–17 with a pair of trailing wheels to carry an enlarged bunker holding 4 tons of coal.

11. Left: Prior to 1896 what is now the western portion of Wykeham Street was known as Reston Street and the two were connected by the wooden footbridge illustrated here.

In 1885 this footbridge caused the town council some concern as they felt that a proper road bridge should be built. They communicated this opinion to the S&W company and received the following reply from the secretary:

"I am desired to write to you in reply that the company will be prepared to provide a footbridge over their railway at Reston Street, of 5 feet in width. As to your enquiry of our engineers relative to the cost of a bridge similar to that at Hibernia Street, the difference between it and that of a footbridge would be, roughly, about £1000 to £1200".

A scheme put forward in 1884 would have changed this scene even more than the appearance of the second Wykeham Street bridge: a line under the title of the Scarborough & East Riding Railway was proposed, which would have connected with the S&WR at this point by a 'Y' junction. The line was intended to go through Driffield and Market Weighton to connect with the Hull & Barnsley Railway at Howden. This would have provided the railways on the west of the Pennines with an east coast outlet independent of the NER which otherwise monopolised rail traffic in the area and the latter strongly opposed the scheme.

£1 Reward.

SCARBOROUGH & WHITBY RAILWAY.

WHEREAS, some evil disposed person or persons, have, between the hours of 5 p.m. on Thursday, the 10th inst., and 6 a.m. on Friday, the 11th inst., wilfully placed a pair of Bogie Wheels on this Railway, near Scarborough Cemetery.

NOTICE IS HEREBY GIVEN, that the above REWARD will be paid to anyone giving such information as will lead to the conviction of the offenders.

Contractor's Office,
Scarborough, May 15th, 1883.

Geo. A. Pindar, Printer, &c., "Advocate" Office, 71, St. Thomas Street, Scarboro.

12. Top left: Hooliganism in 1883, two years before the line opened!

13. Bottom left: The Whitby Moors Rail Tour passing Scarborough cemetery on the final day of passenger traffic on the line on 6th March 1965. The locomotives are class K4 3442 "The Great Marquess" piloting class K1 62005, and both are now preserved. The line on the left is the totally independent track from Gallows Close to the Northstead carriage sidings.

14. Top left: An A8 class locomotive on a train from Whitby in 1954 passing the cemetery footbridge. These engines were introduced by the NER in 1913 with a 4–4–4 wheel arrangement. They were rebuilt from 1931 under the direction of Nigel Gresley and took over from the former class 'W' locomotives on the coast line.

In 1883 a scheme was put forward to run a branch line from here down to the harbour. The line was to go down to the north cliff. where there was to be a station, and thence through Castle Hill. A tramway was to connect with the line at the harbour and run along the foreshore to the Grand Hotel. The proposal fell through due to the lack of financial support from the Harbour Commissioners and the town council who were initially in favour of the scheme. The line would have cost about £74,521 and of this sum the tunnel through Castle Hill would have accounted for £30,000.

It was probably no coincidence that soon after this scheme was proposed, Henry Tennant, the General Manager of the NER, was to be seen on the Scarborough sands questioning the fish merchants as to the charges levied for landing fish as compared with those at other ports.

15. Bottom left: Northstead carriage sidings (also known as Gallows Close carriage sidings) seen from the cemetery footbridge. The independent S&W single track curves round to the right towards Scalby.

The sidings were opened in 1908 in conjunction with Londesborough Road excursion station. They enabled excursion trains to unload at Londesborough Road and run forward through the tunnel up to Northstead where there was a turntable and coaling and watering facilities for the locomotives. This eased the pressure of train movements in Central station and in the evening, when the excursions departed, they could run straight through to Londesborough Road, load up, and be away in minutes.

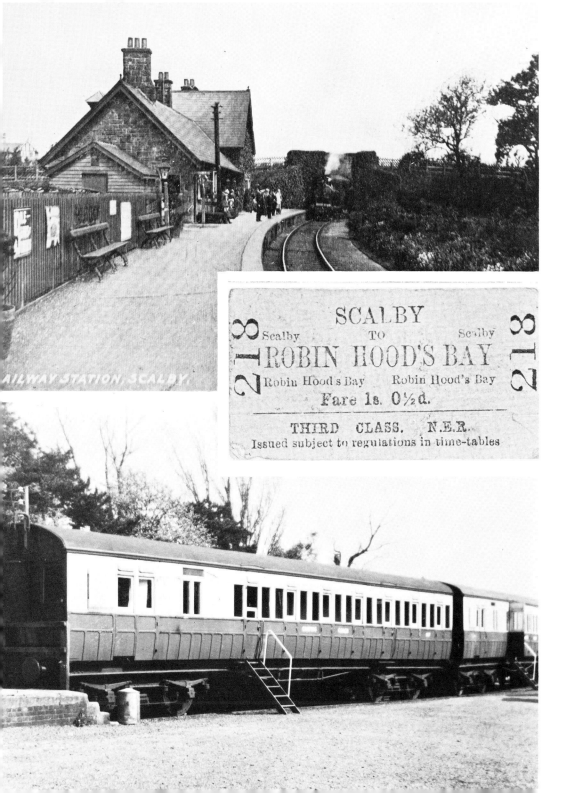

16. Top left: Scalby station from the south at the turn of the century. The whole of the station was demolished in 1974, including the picturesque hump-backed bridge, and the site is now a housing development which incorporates some of the stones from the old station.

The immediate approach to Scalby, from Scarborough, was over a 4-arch brick viaduct which still stands. Originally a cast iron viaduct, completed in 1876, was built by the first contractors, Kirk & Parry. It was demolished in 1881 by Waddells' staff, as it was considered to be too flimsy in construction, and the brick one was built in its place.

In October 1885 the stonemason who placed the coping on the brick viaduct sued Waddell for the sum of £4 13s 10d. He had taken a sub-contract to put up the coping for 8d a foot for squared stones but had been ordered to put chamfered stones on to allow for the vibration of trains (!). He was claiming for 2d a foot more for this work but the contractor counterclaimed, for defective work, and won the case.

Another scheme for a branch railway—the Forge Valley Railway of 1873—would have entailed a junction with the S&WR just short of the south end of the viaduct. The line would have run along the south side of the Scalby cut to Forge Valley through which it would have passed to its termination in West Ayton.

17. Inset: The earliest known ticket from the line dated August 30th 1888, just three years after the line opened.

Train fares on the S&WR in the 1880's were not cheap although they look it by today's standards:

from WHITBY:	1st.	2nd.	3rd.	from SCARBOROUGH:	1st.	2nd.	3rd.
R.H.Bay	1/2d	11d	8d	Scalby	5d	4d	2½d
Fyling Hall	1/4d	1/2d	10d	Cloughton	8d	7d	5d
Peak	1/11d	1/7d	1/1d	Hayburn Wyke	11d	10d	7d
Stainton Dale	2/2d	1/10d	1/3½d	Stainton Dale	1/1d	11d	8d
Hayburn Wyke	2/3d	1/11d	1/4½d	Peak	1/6d	1/3d	10½d
Cloughton	2/6d	2/1d	1/6½d	Fyling Hall	1/11d	1/7d	1/1½d
Scalby	2/10d	2/4d	1/8½d	R.H.Bay	2/2d	1/10d	1/3½d
Scarborough	3/2d	2/8d	1/11d				

For some reason Hawsker was not included in this early fares table.

18. Bottom left: Camping coaches in Scalby station yard in 1958. Five of the eight stations on the line had camping coaches—Scalby (4), Cloughton (3), Stainton Dale (2), Ravenscar (2), and Robin Hood's Bay (5). In addition part of the station buildings at Scalby and Hayburn Wyke were converted into camping cottages when the stations became unstaffed.

SCALBY STATION

ON THE

SCARBOROUGH & WHITBY

RAILWAY

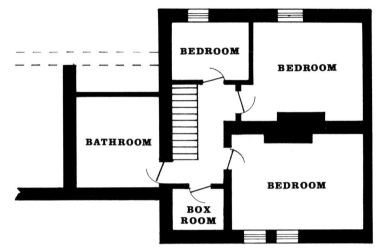

HOUSE: FIRST FLOOR

10   0   10   20   **FEET**

REAR ELEVATION

FRONT ELEVATION

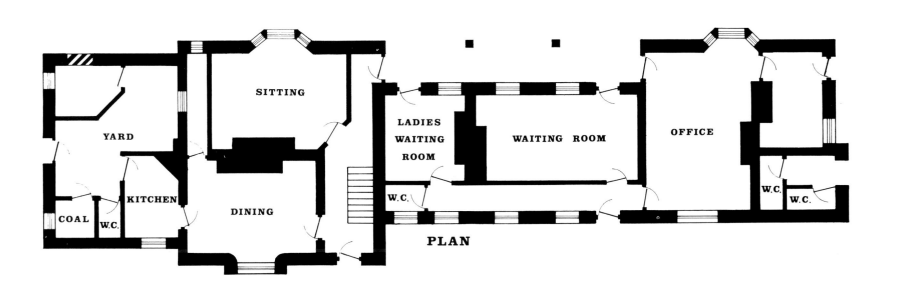

SITTING

YARD

LADIES
WAITING
ROOM

WAITING ROOM

OFFICE

KITCHEN

COAL W.C.

DINING

W.C.

W.C.

W.C.

PLAN

17

19. Left: Scalby station from the north. The building was commenced in January 1885 when it was estimated that it would take two or three months to complete. Like the other stone-built stations on the line (Cloughton, Stainton Dale and Robin Hood's Bay) Scalby was extremely well built—the outer walls were 18 inches thick and of solid stone. There appears to be one basic design but there are some interesting individual variations. The two storey section in all cases is the stationmaster's house (see plans).

Scalby station closed on 2nd February 1953, although certain trains did continue to stop there until 1964 to serve the occupants of the camping coaches.

20. Top right: Cloughton station from the south. On the left is the small goods yard with cattle dock, and goods shed with wooden awning. The main line appears at the bottom left with the passing loop on the right. This was not built until 1891 when the S&WR company authorised the NER to join up what was then a siding to form a complete passing place. The level crossing at the northern end of the station was the only manned one on the line, but when the Government Inspector of the Board of Trade examined the line in 1885, prior to its opening, he stated that the S&WR company should be prepared to build a bridge in its place if this became necessary.

Cloughton became the first place on the line to have a train "service" in January 1884, eighteen months before the line opened officially. This was on the occasion of a Band of Hope meeting at Raven Hall when the contractor fitted out some trucks with seats and the train set off from Scarborough with 80 ladies and gentlemen. At Cloughton they stopped to pick up another 60 although it was to be over a year before the station itself was constructed.

21. Bottom right: Staff at Cloughton station in the 1930's. Left to right: Jack Hanson, Alf Hart, T. McCabe, W. Waugh and Mr J. Waugh, stationmaster at Stainton Dale. Mr Hart became the last stationmaster at Cloughton.

The oil lamp was typical of all the stations on the line and these, together with the office lamps, hand lamps and signal lights, warranted a separate room—the Lamp Room—for their regular preparation and servicing.

22. Top left: Hayburn Wyke from the south. Originally the station was situated on the opposite side of the track but in 1887 the NER complained to the S&WR that:

"This station and the platforms being built of wood are insufficient and of a temporary character. These works must all be built of stone or brick, with sufficient retaining walls, and the platform must be of gravel or other suitable material with stone or cement coping."

As can be seen from this and the next photograph, the station was rebuilt eventually although the buildings were still of wood.

Not all trains were booked to stop here (expresses!) and one driver who made an unscheduled stop at Hayburn Wyke in 1908 was warned to read his Working Timetable, being lucky to get off with only a caution from his superiors.

23. Bottom left: Mr Gooch, stationmaster at Hayburn Wyke in the 1930's. This shows the pride with which most of the stations were looked after by the staff who were often keen gardeners: with only ten trains a day life was far from hectic and there was time enough to cultivate flowers in hanging baskets.

In the distance, on the extreme right, can be seen the stationmaster's house which was built in 1892 at a cost of £330. Prior to this the SM was lodged in a room at the nearby hotel at 5/- a week but had to vacate it when the hotel was fully booked in the summer.

The platform buildings were converted into a camping cottage in the early 1950's and electricity installed for the first time. The stationmaster's office, seen in the foreground, became the living room. The information leaflet for campers intimated that the nearest shops were two miles away at Cloughton, that the beach was 300 feet down a steep cliff and had no sand; the equipment included a heater and two hurricane lamps. . .

The station became an unstaffed halt on 23rd March 1955 under the jurisdiction of the stationmaster at Stainton Dale.

STAINTON DALE STATION.

24. Top left: Staintondale station at the turn of the century. It was from this station in October 1885 that the first consignment of mineral traffic was sent. The load consisted of two trucks of fine building stone from a newly opened quarry, consigned to a Scarborough builder.

In 1887 the NER demanded that a proper and efficient water supply should be provided for the stationmaster's house as the existing one was "unwholesome and precarious" and had been condemned by the medical attendant of the stationmaster's family.

The gradient at Stainton Dale neccessitated the installation of a set of catch points at the southern end of the down loop to prevent vehicles running back onto the single line. In 1899 a driver ran the tender of his engine off the line through these points and was fined 2/6. Drivers at that time were being paid a wage of about 30/- a week.

The name of the station has appeared as "Stainton Dale" and "Staintondale" in the timetables and other publications at various times, and both versions may therefore be considered as correct.

NORTH EASTERN RAILWAY.

PRIZES FOR BEST KEPT WAYSIDE STATIONS, 1922

FIRST CLASS PRIZE

Awarded to **STAINTONDALE** Station.

J. WAUCH _____ Station Master.

R.L. Wrymm General Manager.

25. Bottom left: Many of the stations on the line regularly won the Best Kept Station Certificates of which there were four classes—Special, First, Second and Third. In each class a large number of certificates were awarded except for the Special class of which there were only three. Competition was so keen on the S&WR branch that it developed into a contest to see who could win the specials. In addition to the certificate, which was often proudly displayed at the station, the SM received up to about £10, depending on the class of prize, to share amongst his staff as he thought fit.

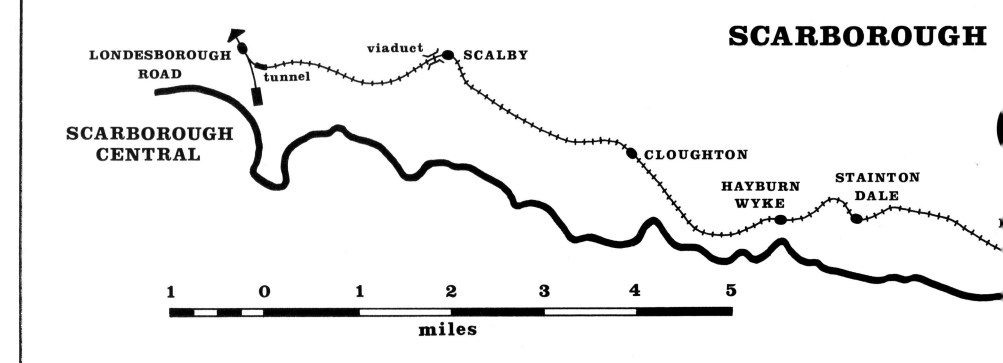

SCARBOROUGH

LONDESBOROUGH
ROAD

SCALBY

viaduct

tunnel

SCARBOROUGH
CENTRAL

CLOUGHTON

HAYBURN
WYKE

STAINTON
DALE

1   0   1   2   3   4   5

miles

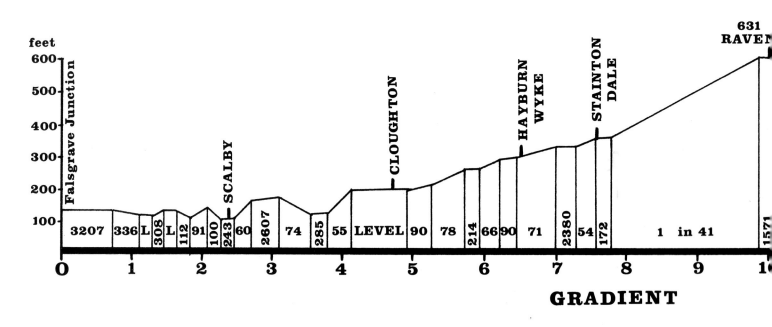

feet

631
RAVEN

Falsgrave Junction

SCALBY

CLOUGHTON

HAYBURN
WYKE

STAINTON
DALE

600
500
400
300
200
100

| 3207 | 336 | L | 308 | L | 112 | 91 | 100 | 243 | 60 | 2607 | 74 | 285 | 55 | LEVEL | 90 | 78 | 214 | 66 | 90 | 71 | 2380 | 54 | 172 | 1 in 41 | 1571 |

0   1   2   3   4   5   6   7   8   9   10

GRADIENT

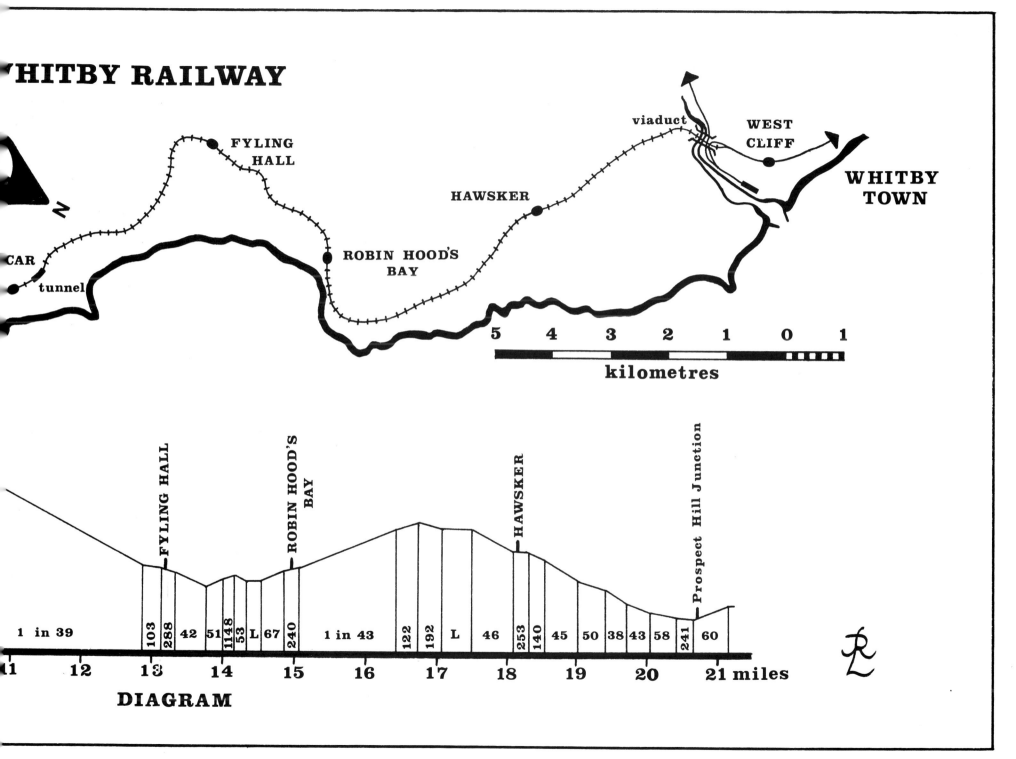

WHITBY RAILWAY

FYLING HALL

HAWSKER

viaduct

WEST CLIFF

WHITBY TOWN

ROBIN HOOD'S BAY

CAR

tunnel

N

5   4   3   2   1   0   1
kilometres

FYLING HALL

ROBIN HOOD'S BAY

HAWSKER

Prospect Hill Junction

1 in 39

103 | 288 | 42 | 51 | 1148 | 53 | L | 67 | 240 | 1 in 43 | 122 | 192 | L | 46 | 253 | 140 | 45 | 50 | 38 | 43 | 58 | 241 | 60

11   12   13   14   15   16   17   18   19   20   21 miles

DIAGRAM

26. Left: A view from the north end of the down platform at Stainton Dale showing some of the more familiar examples of station hardware.

The signals are typical of the once common NER slotted-post type. The signal arm is pivoted within a slot in the wide section of the post. Even in this modest country station the signal cabin had 15 working levers. Seven of these controlled the signals themselves, the others operated the points and the intricate interlocking system that ensured, as far as it was mechanically possible, that the points at the opposite ends of the passing loop could not be set for conflicting routes. They also interlocked with the signals in order to protect locomotives shunting in the goods yard.

"THE STATION RAVENSCAR"

27. Top left: Ravenscar station from the south. The station was called "Peak", from the opening in 1885, but was re-named Ravenscar on 1st October 1897. Originally, as this photograph of 1907 shows, the station had only a single track and a goods siding.

A stationmaster's house was lacking, as was the case at Hayburn Wyke, and in 1886 the NER pressed the S&WR company to provide one. By 1895 a house had still not been built and the NER, in retaliation, closed Peak station on the 6th of March. The S&W board, after some more prevarication, finally agreed to pay for one and the station was reopened, appropriately, on the 1st April 1896.

28. Bottom left: In 1908 a passing loop was built at Ravenscar and a wooden platform and waiting room erected. They are seen here from the north in Wolrd War I with a train arriving from Scarborough.

The first excursion to Peak took place in January 1884 when 140 people attended a Band of Hope meeting at Raven Hall (see photograph 20). In the same year a 29 year old navvy was killed by a fall of clay whilst excavating in one of the cuttings. A police constable was killed in the same year whilst riding on a ballast train near here. He was on one of the end trucks which became detached on the steep gradient and in attempting to apply the brake he was suddenly thrown off. He was 36, married, and resided in the company's property at Scarborough where he had lived for two years.

In May 1885 another excursion took place, this time for a temperence meeting, when a train of three covered carriages left Scarborough, arriving at Peak at 3-30, having taken an hour for the ten mile journey. The Rev. Balgarnie of Scarborough, who had recently returned from America, addressed the meeting and said that the workmen's shanties at Peak reminded him of the far west settlements of America where a school and a church were generally the first buildings to be erected; here they had erected a hall which combined the gospel and temperance thus taking cognizance of the bodies and souls of the workmen.

25

29. Above: The north end of Ravenscar station in 1957. Mr. J. S. Tidey takes the tablet (see inside back cover, photograph 58) to the driver of a down train. On the extreme right is the post indicating the severe 1 in 39 gradient down through the tunnel to Fyling Hall. "Peak" was certainly a more appropriate name for the station as the gradient on the south side down to Stainton Dale is almost as bad at 1 in 41. The weather here in winter can be nothing short of atrocious with extremely high winds—strong enough to blow the horns off a bullock, according to one SM. The wooden waiting room did in fact once blow away.

30. Above: The south end of the 279 yard long Ravenscar tunnel in 1945 with an A8 class locomotive, 2161, bound for Scarborough.

A tunnel was completed here in 1876 by the first contractors, Kirk & Parry, but was later discovered to be partly on the wrong course and was rebuilt in 1883/4. In fact a tunnel was not necessary—it would have been easier to make a cutting—but W. H. Hammond, of Raven Hall, objected and insisted that a tunnel should be built through his land. The S&WR board agreed and gave their engineer instructions to have the tunnel built at an additional cost of £500. It was completed in October 1884. W. H. Hammond died in October 1885, having lived just long enough to learn that his brainchild had at last been opened to the public.

31. Top left: Whitaker's brickworks situated in the old alum quarries a short distance to the north of the tunnel. The brickworks were opened in about 1900 and produced bricks on which was stamped the word RAVENSCAR.

Although the gradient up from Fyling Hall to the summit, (about three miles) is a nominal 1 in 39, there is a definite easing at this point. One old engine driver used sometimes to stop here so that his fireman could raise a good head of steam to blast their way through the tunnel to Ravenscar as they would not risk getting stuck.

32. Bottom left: An unusual view taken in about 1920 of the embankment over Stoupe Beck just south of Fyling Hall Station. This is the largest embankment on the line, being 90 feet high and 300 feet across at the base. It was the last one to be built in Fylingdales and in August 1884 it was reported that about 490,000 cubic yards of earthwork had been tipped to form the embankments in this area and two locomotives were running between here and Peak bringing burnt shale from the alum workings to form the Stoupe Beck embankment.

33. Top left: Fyling Hall station from the Boggle Hole road bridge. An example of one of the typical complaints about timetables and facilities arose in connection with Fyling Hall, in 1886, when a Mr John Popple wrote to the S&WR company:

"Yesterday I had occasion to meet Mr John Frank of Pickering at Sleights station at 8-44am to go to Fylingdales for the purpose of selling him 16 acres of timber. On our arrival at Whitby we found the next train to leave for that district (Fylingdales) was 11-46am and we must either stay 3 hours in Whitby or take a trap, this latter we were compelled to do to get our business done. After we had gone through the several woods we next found our way to Fyling Hall station and there the stationmaster told us that he was not allowed to take any timber at his station, although there is plenty of room, and with very little trouble every convenience could be made. The loss to the Owners of the Timber is this, that the cost of the carriage by road to Hawsker the nearest available station would be so much that the Timber would not be worth felling, and of course it will be a loss to the company in carriage if the wood cannot be conveyed. I should have at least 300 tons to go from this station . . ."

Perhaps the sylvan setting would not have existed if the facilities had been made available.

34. Bottom left: Fyling Hall from the south, one of the four stations without a passing loop. The Committee on Coast Line Working suggested that a passing place could be provided here in 1934 at a cost of about £3500 but this was rejected due to the short seasonal duration of traffic.

Fyling Hall was made into a Block Post at the Committee's recommendation in 1934. This enabled two trains to be on the line between Ravenscar and Robin Hood's Bay (travelling in the same direction). Mr A. T. Hart remembers delivering the Block instrument to the station in a rather unusual manner. He stood on the front of a locomotive, hanging onto the smokebox door handle with one hand whilst steadying the apparatus at his feet with the other— a somewhat hair raising ride down the 1 in 39 gradient.

The station was converted into an unstaffed halt on 5 May 1958.

35. Top left: At the time this photograph was taken, in the late 1940's, Albert Hunter was signalman at Fyling Hall and responsible for this superb show of flowers. In the height of summer he had great difficulty in seeing out of the signal box (right of centre). Mr Hunter was noted for his gardening skills and was a regular winner of the Best Kept Station Certificates. Whilst stationed at Staintondale in the early 1930's he stayed up very late one night to tidy the station prior to an inspection: he overslept the next morning and stopped the first train which was supposed to go straight through!

36. Bottom left: An aspect of the line that few visitors saw but many residents had to contend with—Fyling Hall during a severe winter. The locomotive would be lucky to reach Ravenscar.

In February/March 1886 there were severe snowfalls which blocked the line completely. These were cleared by Waddell's staff at a cost of £78 14s 2d and the bill was sent to the NER. They would not pay it as they maintained that it was the S&WR company's responsibility, contrary to the Articles of the Working Agreement. In order to obtain payment Waddell deducted the amount from a bill which he owed to the NER for the signalling at Prospect Hill. In their turn the NER took the unwarranted step of deducting the sum from the S&WR company's share of the traffic returns.

37. Right: A superb photograph taken by the late Dr C. C. Cobb in 1945 between Fyling Hall and Robin Hood's Bay. The locomotive, number 7276, is one of the G5 class which worked many of the trains on the line.

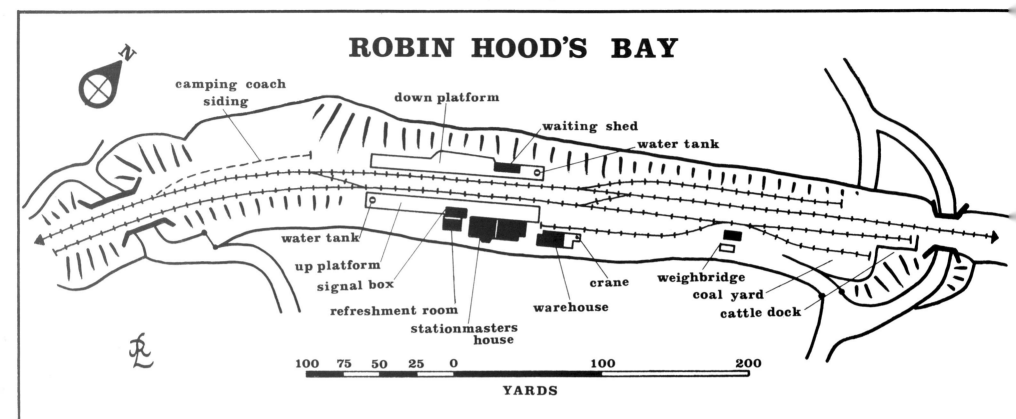

ROBIN HOOD'S BAY

camping coach siding
down platform
waiting shed
water tank
water tank
up platform
signal box
refreshment room
stationmasters house
warehouse
crane
weighbridge
coal yard
cattle dock

100 75 50 25 0   100   200

YARDS

THE FIRST TRAIN SERVICE: 16th. to 31st. JULY 1885

	am	pm	pm	pm		am	am	pm	pm
SCARBOROUGH	9-10	1-0	5-0	8-15	WHITBY West Cliff	7-40	11-35	3-10	6-45
Scalby	9-18	1-8	5-8	8-23	Hawsker	7-51	11-46	3-21	6-56
Cloughton	9-24	1-14	5-14	8-29	Robin Hood's Bay	8-2	11-57	3-32	7-7
Hayburn Wyke	9-30	1-20	5-20	8-35	Fyling Hall	8-9	12-4	3-39	7-14
Staintondale	9-35	1-25	5-25	8-40	Peak	8-19	12-14	3-49	7-24
Peak	9-43	1-33	5-33	8-48	Staintondale	8-26	12-21	3-56	7-31
Fyling Hall	9-53	1-43	5-43	8-58	Hayburn Wyke	8-31	12-26	4-1	7-36
Robin Hood's Bay	9-58	1-48	5-48	9-3	Cloughton	8-37	12-32	4-7	7-42
Hawsker	10-10	1-58	5-58	9-13	Scalby	8-43	12-38	4-13	7-48
WHITBY West Cliff	10-20	2-10	6-10	9-25	SCARBOROUGH	8-50	12-45	4-20	7-55

38. Top right: Robin Hood's Bay station from the south-west in 1957, with the late R. E. Ascough, the last stationmaster. Construction here was not without incident, as is illustrated by the following extract from the Scarborough Gazette of 24th April 1884:

"A serious riot occurred on Saturday night at Robin Hood's Bay near Whitby. A number of navvies who had been drinking quarelled and fought. The police interfeared(sic), and the combatants then turned upon the constables. A general melee ensued in which Police Constable Lazenby was knocked down and brutally kicked. Eventually the police were assisted by some civilians and three of the rioters were arrested. A number of constables and navvies were wounded".

39. Bottom right: Engine 1679 on an inspection saloon at Robin Hood's Bay in 1921. In the foreground can be seen the commencement of the goods yard sidings: these are the original rails and chairs laid down in 1884. The chief characteristic of *inside* wooden keys can clearly be seen. The cast iron chairs were especially made for the S&WR, see photograph 45.

A driver and fireman who left their cattle stock special train in the goods yard on a hot summer day in 1903 slaked their thirst in the nearest hostelry and came back rather the worse for wear. The driver was suspended for a week and the fireman for a month. The driver, who was born in 1865, had started work at the age of 13 in 1878 as an engine cleaner for the NER, earning 1/8d a week.

NORTH EASTERN RAILWAY.

HALF-DAY EXCURSION

To Robin Hood's Bay and Whitby.

On Tuesday, July 4th,

An Excursion train will run as under, to

ROBIN HOOD'S BAY

AND

WHITBY,

Returning from Whitby (West Cliff) at 8-45 p.m.,
and Robin Hood's Bay at 9-5 p.m. same day.

	p.m.	Fares there and back, Third Class.	
		To Robin Hood's Bay.	To Whitby.
Scarbro' dep.	1 25		
Scalby „	1 35	**1/3**	**1/6**
Cloughton „	1 42		

Children not exceeding 3, free; above 3 and under 12 years of age, half-fare.

A limited number of carriages will be provided for this Excursion, and in order as far as possible to secure the comfort of the passengers and to avoid delay, the issue of tickets will be limited to the carriage accommodation provided, and passengers who intend to travel by the train should therefore apply early for such tickets, which can now be obtained at the above-mentioned stations.

The tickets issued at the above fares are only available for the Excursion train from and to the stations at and for which they are issued, and are not transferable, and no passenger will be allowed to leave the train at any intermediate station. Passengers travelling by this train without having first obtained a ticket for it, will be required to pay the ordinary single fare.

NO LUGGAGE ALLOWED.

York, June, 1898.　　　　**GEORGE S. GIBB, General Manager.**

Ben Johnson & Co., Printers, York.—No. 288—27-6-98.

THE MOUNT PLEASANT BUILDING ESTATE

Robin Hood's Bay,

YORKSHIRE,

Affords splendid Sites close to the sea for the erection of superior Villa Residences or high-class Boarding or Lodging Houses.

The unique little Town of Robin Hood's Bay is widely known for its quaint picturesqueness.

The position of the Estate is exceptionally attractive. It commands extensive views not only over the sea but also of the lovely scenery of this the most beautiful part of the Yorkshire Coast. It is protected on the North by the high moorlands; the soil is dry and the climate invigorating.

The Robin Hood's Bay Station of the Scarborough and Whitby Railway is within 200 yards of the Estate, which is therefore extremely convenient for residences of gentlemen engaged in business in either of those towns.

The Estate is divided into 52 Lots of convenient size. Good supplies of gas and water are available.

The roads have been or will be completely made and sewered by the Vendors.

The purchase money may, if preferred, be paid by quarterly instalments extending over five years.

Full particulars, with plans and conditions of Sale, may be had from MESSRS. JOHN HETHERTON & CO., Exchange Chambers, Clifford Street, York; MR. ALEXANDER WILSON, Scarborough and Whitby Railway Offices, Scarborough; or from MESSRS. WELLS & HIND, Solicitors, Nottingham.

40. Left: Ephemera. An excursion handbill of 1893 and the advertisement on the back cover of the Official S&WR Guide of 1894 (see photograph 2).

41. Top right: A Sentinel railcar at the "up" platform at Robin Hood's Bay. This is the same car that appears in photograph 8, also taken on 6th April 1927. Here it had just arrived from Whitby with a horse box in tow to test its hauling capabilities.

On the 7th May 1928 another Sentinel railcar was tested on the line and acceleration tests were made on the gradient from Fyling Hall up to Ravenscar. The car, which weighed 31 tons 15 cwt in working order, was loaded to 33 tons: equivalent to about 16 passengers with luggage. From a standing start at Fyling Hall a speed of about 21 mph was quickly attained on the 1 in 103 gradient, but on the 1 in 39 gradient the speed dropped to an average of 14½ mph and the three mile journey took 12 minutes.

42. Bottom right: The shelter on the down platform at Robin Hood's Bay was fairly typical of NER construction, although the majority were fully enclosed to give complete protection from the weather.

An unusual practical and somewhat macabre joke was played on unsuspecting passengers at this station. It came about because of the local branch of the St. John's Ambulance Brigade holding its classes in the waiting room. One of the items used for instruction was a complete articulated human skeleton which was kept in a box under the waiting room table. The local youngsters used to extract "Charlie" from his box and suspend him in the waiting room doorway prior to the departure of a train load of holidaymakers. One dry wit remarked that "he" looked as though he had been waiting a long time.

43, 44, 45. Left: Hawsker was the only station built of brick although the design is very similar to that of the stone-built stations. The upper photograph shows 69879, class A8, about to pick up the tablet on its way through to Whitby.

In the list of unfinished works which the NER sent to the S&WR by way of complaint in 1887 there appeared the following reference with regard to Hawsker station:

"The present House for the Station Master has been declared by the Sanitary Authority, and is, unfit for habitation, this must be remedied, either by erecting a new house with accommodation equal to that provided at Fyling-hall, or by satisfactorily altering and improving the present House, so as to meet the approval of the Sanitary Authority".

The lower photograph reveals a view rarely seen by the public—the interior of Hawsker booking office in 1964. The photograph could have been taken 50 years earlier.

In the centre at the back is the ticket window with its vertically sliding door; immediately to the right is the ticket rack in which at least 18 different types of ticket are visible. On the extreme left end of the counter is the ticket dating instrument, and in front of the ticket window a fine oil lamp from the days before the station was supplied with electricity. On the right are the parcels scales and, above, the tables of charges.

The upright photograph is of a S&W rail chair (see also photograph 39). These chairs were cast in 1883 by Wilson, Pease & Co. and were designed to use double bull-headed rail weighing 75 lb/yard which after wearing on the upper surface could be turned over to use the other head. Unfortunately this theory did not work in practice as the rails wore where they rested on the chairs and, when turned, resulted in a rough ride for passengers. Most of the track would have been replaced after a few years but some of it remained in the sidings at Cloughton and Hawsker until closure. This example was discovered at Hawsker by Alf Wilson in 1973, when the final stretch of track between Bog Hall (at Whitby) and Hawsker was removed. The rest of the line was lifted in 1968 but this section had been left in for possible use in connection with a proposed potash mine at Hawsker Bottoms.

46. Right: (Crown Copyright). An aerial view of the Esk Viaduct and Prospect Hill area to the south-west of Whitby. The line from Hawsker enters the picture at the bottom right and curves up to cross the Esk Viaduct in the centre. From here the line curves to the left passing under a narrow footbridge to Prospect Hill. The junction of the S&W line with the former Whitby, Redcar & Middlesbrough Union Railway line can be seen just below the wide road bridge near the top of the photograph. Half way between the two bridges the burnt out remains of Prospect Hill signal box can just be pinpointed. The WR&MUR line which comes into the photograph at the top left, from West Cliff station, passed under the signal box on a falling gradient and curved to pass under the northern end of the viaduct to join the Whitby-Pickering line at Bog Hall by the river Esk. The W&P line passes out of the photograph at the bottom left.

The line at Larpool Woods, in the lower right, was the site of an extraordinary scene in July 1884 when a locomotive was delivered to work on this section before the viaduct was finished. The engine was taken from the NER at Ruswarp and hauled up the road to Larpool by a team of 19 horses.

47. Top left: Class A8, 9881, leaves the south end of the Esk viaduct with a passenger train for Scarborough in 1947.

48. Bottom left: An early view of the Esk viaduct from Larpool. The construction of the viaduct commenced on 17th October 1882 and took almost exactly two years: the first locomotive passed over it on 24th October 1884.

The viaduct is 915 feet long, 125 feet high from the river bed to the parapet and is estimated to contain about 5 million bricks. It is supported by 12 piers and there are 13 arches each with an average span of 60 feet. The largest span is 64 feet over the centre of the river. Six piers at the southern end and three at the north end are square with the structure but the other three are on the "skew" so that they do not deflect the course of the river, which is tidal at this point. Although the viaduct is straight for most of its length the northern end terminates by a ten chain curve. The weight of the structure is estimated at 25,700 tons and it cost approximately £40,000.

Behind the northern end of the viaduct can be seen the last two bridges on the S&WR, numbers 61 and 62; this gives the rather high average of three bridges per mile, in addition to which there are a number of culverts of some magnitude (Stoupe Beck).

49. Top right: In 1884 the noted Whitby photographer, Frank M, Sutcliffe, visited the Esk viaduct and took photographs of it under construction. The viaduct was the most important engineering structure on the line and Waddell employed a large staff here. together with some of the most sophisticated equipment of the day. Materials were brought in on a specially built siding connected to the Whitby-Pickering line on the far side of the river.

Before commencing construction borings were taken on the proposed site of each pier in order to determine the depth at which the bedrock lay, as it is overlain by silt and boulder clay at this point. Solid rock was reached at a depth of about 42 feet below the river bed and no obstructions were discovered.

50. Bottom right: The principal difficulty was in sinking the cylinders of brickwork to support the four piers in the river. Each pier is supported on three of these cylinders which are each 14 feet in diameter. At the base of each is a wrought iron cutting shoe six feet high (seen in the centre of the photograph) which was placed in position on the river bed at low tide. The brickwork was then built up on this and a grab used to remove the silt and clay from the inside. The brick cylinders then sank under their own weight although Charles Fox, the engineer recalled that they would often reach quite a height before they sank, sometimes up to 20 feet at a time, usually on an incoming tide.

51. Top left: When the cylinders reached a depth of about 30 feet they started hitting obstructions which turned out to be a quantity of oak tree trunks lying on their sides, some of which were up to three feet in diameter. A diver (seen on the left holding his helmet) had then to go down inside the cylinder with hammer and chisel, and a saw, to cut through the trunks. Before he could do this he had to excavate a hole under the obstruction, climb into it, and then, with a few tons of brickwork poised above his head, partially cut through the wood until the grab could break it off. This difficult feat was accomplished many times and without a single accident. Once bedded on the rock the cylinders were partially filled with concrete and connected together at the top by jack arches (seen in photograph 48) and the whole structure levelled off to form a base for the pier.

Large piles of S&W rail chairs can be seen steadying the supports for the grabs.

52. Bottom left: Waddell's gang at the south end of the viaduct. There are 49 masons, navvies and other staff on this photograph taken by Sutcliffe in the latter half of 1884, the masons proudly displaying their trowels.

On the left is the wooden framework, known as the centreing, upon which the brickwork of the arches is built.

A contemporary account of the viaduct on its completion described it as "architecturally unique and unlike many structures of similar magnitude in other places, adds grandeur and beauty to the locality in which it is placed".

It was designed by C. A. Rowlandson of the firm of Charles Fox & Sons, Engineers, a Mr. Walter Gowans was the engineer in charge and the foreman of the works was Mr. Pickard. A navvy's pay at this time was from about 2/4d. to 2/8d. for a 10 hour day.

53. Right: The approaches to Prospect Hill in 1945. The Esk viaduct can be seen at the top centre with the S&W line coming under the footbridge to the left. A train for Scarborough climbs the 1 in 50 gradient from Whitby Town to West Cliff where the engine will reverse.

54. Top left: Prospect Hill from the south. The former WR&MUR climbs up to West cliff on the left. On the right the S&W line, with a passing loop, descends to join the former below the road bridge.

In 1882 the directors of the S&WR asked the secretary to write to Mr. Wise, the company's land agent, to instruct him to buy sufficient land at Whitby for a small independent station. They had however already refused a petition from the ratepayers of Whitby for a station at Larpool on the grounds that the gradient was too steep. The only site near Whitby which could have accommodated a station was probably this one at Prospect Hill.

55. Bottom left: Prospect Hill signal box. This was an unusual type for this area and was necessitated by the deep cutting in which the lines ran. It commanded an excellent view of both the Whitby-Saltburn line, below, and the S&W line which ran above the retaining wall on the right.

An account for the signalling work was rendered to the S&WR company by the NER on 20th July 1886 and amounted to £644 7s. 3d. This would probably include the signal box itself.

56. Right: Engine 957 (LNER class X2) with an inspection saloon at Prospect Hill in 1903/4. The locomotive was built in 1874 as an 0–4—4T and rebuilt into this form (2–2–4T) in 1903. For many years it was based at Hull where it was occasionally allowed to take out a two-coach passenger train to York.

7 A 9 5

57. Left: Prospect Hill from the north. The S&WR terminates in the foreground by a junction with the line from Whitby Town to Loftus.

The retaining walls were completed in February 1884 and the rails and points for the junction fixed in June of that year. In May 1881, when a few miles of the WR&MUR had been built at the Whitby end, it was suggested that there should be a combined WR&MUR/S&WR station at Whitby. The two companies were later to form a Joint Committee with offices in the S&WR property at 1, West Parade, Scarborough. This was to try and sort out their joint grievances with the NER, but Henry Tennant refused to recognise their right to form such a committee.